BUT IT DOESN'T AFFECT ME

Go for it.

BUT IT DOESN'T AFFECT ME

LEARNING TO THINK FOR YOURSELF

Al Menconi

NEW SONG PUBLISHING

A division of Al Menconi Ministries
Carlsbad, CA 92013

www.AlMenconi.com

But It Doesn't Affect Me
Al Menconi

NEW SONG
PUBLISHING

New Song Publishing
A Division of Al Menconi Ministries
Carlsbad, CA 92013
www.AlMenconi.com

First Printing 2003
Second Printing 2005
Third Printing 2009
©2005/2006, ©2009/2010 Al Menconi Ministries

Cover and interior design & production: Mark Rayburn, Rayburn Design

ISBN 978-0-942925-12-8

Printed in the United States of America.

ACKNOWLEDGEMENTS

I thank my wife, Jan, and daughters, Ann and Allison, who continue to teach me how to become the husband and father God has called me to be.

I thank my good friend, Joyce Ross, who never gave up on me—even when no one else gave me a prayer.

I thank Tim LaHaye for teaching me who I am, why I'm here, where I am going, and what is truth.

I thank my pastor, Rick Myatt, for being such a wonderful example of a godly teacher with balance and common sense.

I thank my good friend, Mike Yorkey, for encouraging me to develop this book for a wider audience.

I thank all my former students, especially the class of '78 from Christian High, for challenging me to continue to give a reason for what I believe.

I thank Adina Jaitly, my assistant and trusted "right hand," who challenged every concept and has helped me put this book together.

I thank Mark Rayburn, who took my silly little book of clip art and line drawings and designed it into this challenging book that God is using to change lives for His Kingdom.

Most of all, I thank Jesus Christ who took my lost worthless soul and gave me a worthwhile purpose because of His cross and resurrection.

INTRODUCTION

DID YOU EVER WONDER HOW SOMEONE IS "ON FIRE" FOR JESUS ONE MOMENT AND A FEW MONTHS LATER THAT SAME PERSON ISN'T EVEN SURE IF THERE IS A GOD?

HAVE YOU EVER HAD A "MOUNTAIN TOP EXPERIENCE," BUT CAN'T FIGURE OUT WHY YOU SPEND MOST OF YOUR LIFE IN THE "VALLEY?"

HAVE YOU EVER TRIED LIVING FOR JESUS, BUT YOU JUST CAN'T SEEM TO DO ANYTHING RIGHT?

DO YOU EVER FEEL THAT EVERYONE IS HAVING A "GOOD TIME" BUT YOU?

I can't guarantee that this book will answer all of these questions—that isn't my goal. My goal for this book is to encourage you to think for yourself. I will not tell you what to think, rather, give you questions to equip you to learn how to think for yourself.

Ultimately, life is a series of choices. What are you going to choose?

My hope and prayer is that you will read this book with an open mind and an open heart.

—Al Menconi

CHAPTER ONE

One time, while on a **FLIGHT BACK EAST, I** began talking to a **young man** who was sitting **next to me** on the plane.

It turned out that **WE** had both attended a Marilyn Manson **CONCERT,** and we had an interesting CONVERSATION about it.

He thought
the **CONCERT**
was GREAT.

CONCERT
CONCERT
CONCERT

I had a different **opinion.**

But I **DIDN'T** want to
turn him off, so I just **listened**

AND didn't offer my opinion

OPINION OPINION OPINION

...at first.

A few minutes into the conversation, **I TOLD HIM** that *I attended the concert* as a **CONCERNED CHRISTIAN.**

HIS DEFENSES WENT UP.

He protested, *"IT DOESN'T AFFECT ME!"* *"IT DOESN'T AFFECT ME!"* You could almost see him **THROW HIS HANDS UP in self-defense!**

He acted as if
I was getting ready to attack him
and he had to
DEFEND
HIMSELF.

Obviously, other Christians
he had met had tried to

CRAM

their opinion
of his music
DOWN his throat.

Since I was a Christian,
he expected me to condemn him too.
But I didn't.
I simply asked:

"**What doesn't affect you?**"

"WHAT DOESN'T AFFECT YOU?"

"Whatdoesn'taffectyou?"

"Whatdoesn'taffectyou?"

"Marilyn Manson.*

His music
doesn't affect me!"

He replied,
quite sure of himself.

*Marilyn Manson—a shock-rocker of the last century.

His music doesn't affect me!

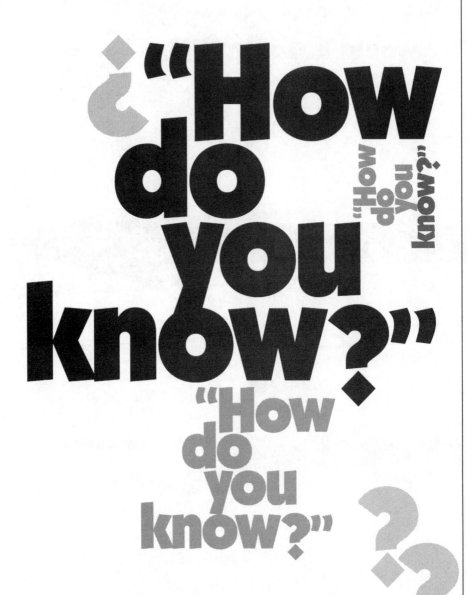

I didn't realize
the **EFFECT**
this **simple question**
would have on **HIM.**
You could almost **see**
the RUST coming out of his
ears
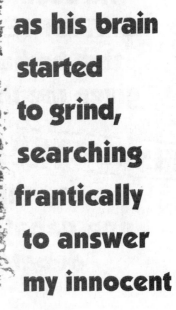
as his brain
started
to grind,
searching
frantically
to answer
my innocent
little
QUESTION.

"Well, I'm not a
Satanist!"
he said finally.

He seemed
SATISFIED
that he had
given me the

FINAL ANSWER

to this
non-debate
debate.

His reasoning seemed logical.
"Marilyn Manson is a Satanist.
I listen to Marilyn Manson, but
I haven't become a Satanist.
Therefore,
   his music must not affect me."

"Marilyn Manson isn't a Satanist either!"
                           I replied.

You could see the
look of surprise on his face.

"He plays with occult images
and he's a sexual pervert,
but he's NOT a Satanist."

"Then he's okay to listen to, right?

He quickly sidestepped from being defensive to looking for an excuse.

"It depends,

...Would you rather be locked in a little room with a Satanist or a SEXUAL PERVERT?"

When he **laughed**
HA HA HA ha ha ha

at my response,

I could see he was just LOOK**I**NG

for a reasonable answer.

As we talked, he let his **DEFENSES** down,

and we were able to

have *NORMAL* conversation.

How about you?

How would

you

respond

to a

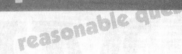

reasonable question

about your

Does your

ENTER TAIN MENT

ENTERTAINMENT

affect you?

¿¿¿
¿¿¿
¿¿¿
¿¿¿
¿¿¿
¿¿¿
¿¿¿
¿¿¿

How do you know?

??
??
??
??
??
??
??
??

Could the Bible
have a reasonable answer
to your entertainment?

What would you do if 𝕲𝖔𝖉 sat down next to you and told you that...

DUDE...
YOUR ENTERTAINMENT
LIKE, HURTS ME.

...your entertainment hurts Him?

Would You Care?

would i care? ME?? care??

How about if

asked you to

change your

WOULD YOU

**I'm not saying
your entertainment
has any effect
on your life
one way or another,
but would you
be interested in seeing
what the Bible says?**

CHAPTER TWO

Since you made it this far,
I assume you want to see
what **Scripture** says
about your ENTERTAINMENT.

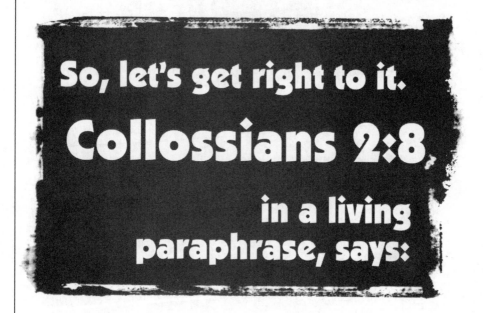

So, let's get right to it.
Collossians 2:8,
in a living
paraphrase, says:

"'"Don't let others spoil your Faith and Joy with their Philosophies., their wrong and shallow answers. . .,"

.....BASED ON MEN"S
THOUGHTS AND IDEAS
INSTEAD OF ON WHAT
CHRIST HAS SAID."'"

Hey! I have
an idea...

Think about it! Isn't the vast majority of today's entertainment based on some man's or woman's thoughts and ideas?

Isn't rock music, or any other style of music, simply some man's or woman's thoughts and ideas written as lyrics and set to a tune?

Aren't motion pictures, television programs, and videos simply some man's or woman's thoughts and ideas put on celluloid and then shown on a screen?

Have you ever thought about this?

Before Grand Theft Auto and other video games became so popular, they were somebody's **thoughts and ideas.**

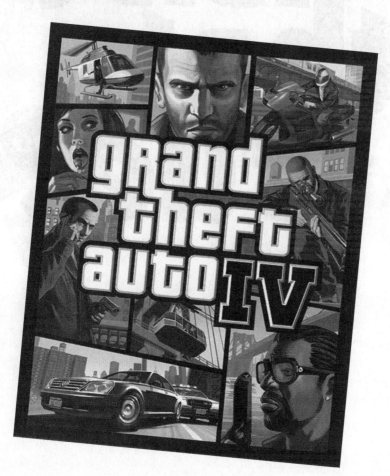

Isn't that true?

So what?

So what? So what? So what? S

The Bible says you will spoil your FAITH and JOY if you keep shoving the empty philosophies of this world into your mind.

That's what!

With so much of today's entertainment based on thoughts and ideas that are against what the Bible has to say, it seems reasonable to ask the following questions:

- **How is your faith in Jesus Christ?**
- **Do you ever think you've lost your salvation?**
- **Do you wonder if there is a God?**
- **Is Jesus God?**
- **Is the Bible true?**
- **Do you ever have problems with your faith?**

¿No?

That's Great!

How's your JOY?

Do you have...

- Love
- Joy
- Peace
- Gentleness
- Kindness
- Hope
- Patience
- etc. etc...

That's part of the Fruit of the Spirit.

Galatians 5:22+23

"But the fruit of the Spirit is...
love,
joy,
peace,
patience,
kindness,
goodness,
faithfulness, gentleness,
and Self Control..."

All together they are called JOY.

Does JOY radiate in your life?

No?

Why not?

Why not?

Maybe you have been
allowing someone else
to undermine

your
Faith in Jesus

And the

JOY of your Salvation

through their
Philosophies.

CHAPTER 3 THREE

Did **YOU** realize that when you committed your life to **Christ** and joined the

Kingdom of Light,
that...
Satan declared war on you?

The Daily Transcript

The People's News Choice for Over 130 Years — Afternoon Final

Sunday, Just Before the War

SATAN DECLARES WAR!

Another Human Accepts Jesus— Satan Opens Fire.

Denver, CO—People who accept Jesus are subject to a subtle but dangerous attack when they least expect it to happen. Today, while playing

It's a spiritual war for your mind.

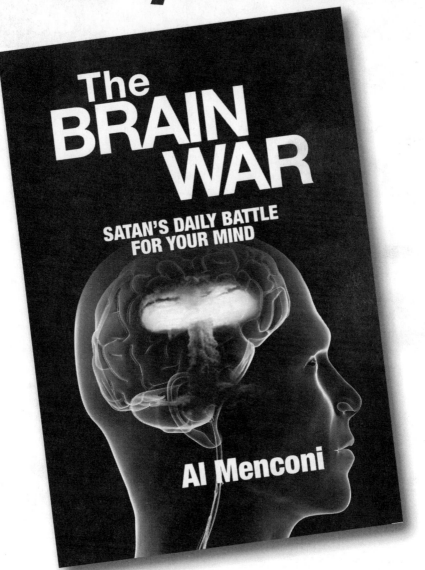

Most Christians DON'T REALIZE they are in a **war for control** of their mind.

If they knew what Satan was doing, they would set up some defenses and **BE READY** for him.

knew

knew

If I knew...

Knew what?

BUT he isn't going to warn you that you are in a WAR.

He's just going to start shooting.

And he aims his **ammunition**
(his philosophies)
FROM
the most unsuspecting

PLACES.

AND... A FEW OBVIOUS PLACES.

He uses
much of today's
ENTERTAINMENT MEDIA
as weapons
aimed
directly
at our
Faith and Joy.

The world of ENTERTAINMENT isn't the only battlefield, but it's one of the most important ones especially to young people!

Is Satan winning THiS BATTLE for in your life?

REMEMBER!

REMEMBER!
IMPORTANTE!
REMEMBER!

DON'T FORGET!

Satan hates you!

- He would destroy you completely if he could.

- But he can't.
  God won't let him.

- So he uses sneaky tricks on us.

- Since he can't destroy our Christianity, he'll settle for **weakening** it instead.

CHAPTER FOUR

When I first became a Christian, I expected to be covered in so much of God's goodness and rightness that I would be PERFECT.

I wasn't.

I tried to be "good" but I couldn't stop thinking and doing things that I knew wouldn't make God happy. When I realized I wasn't perfect, I started to wonder if God had come into my life at all!

At first I didn't realize that this was:

one of Satan's best tricks to fool Christians.

best tricks best tricks

Hey, watch this one.

Then I read what the Bible had to say in Romans 8:38-39

"For I am convinced that neither death nor life, neither angels nor demons, neither the present nor the future, nor any powers, neither height nor depth, nor anything else in all creation, will be able to separate us from the love of God that is in Christ Jesus our Lord."

GOD

WILL

NEVER

LEAVE

US!

EVER.

I found out
when we commit
our life to Jesus,
He will never
forsake us or leave us.

NOTHING can separate us from the love of

God.

NOTHING!

USLOVEUSOFUSGOD
USLOVEUSOFUSGOD
USLOVEUSOFUSGOD
USLOVEUSOFUSGOD
USLOVEUSOFUSGOD
USLOVEUSOFUSGOD
USLOVEUSOFUSGOD
USLOVEUSOFUSGOD

We have been transferred from the kingdom of darkness to the kingdom of

LIGHT

Read Colossians 1:13

"'FOR HE DELIVERED US FROM THE POWER OF DARKNESS, AND TRANSFERRED US INTO THE KINGDOM OF HIS SON!'"

You can look it up for yourself. Colossians is close to the middle of the New Testament, Just after Philippians and just before I Thessalonians.

Satan has lost us
FOREVER!

He CAN'T get us back.

So the next best thing he can do is to make us

ineffective **and**

Weak

weak

not strong

I feel weak

puny

I'm not strong

What makes a Christian STRONG?

Nehemiah 8:10 says...

It's not just
the *title* of a song
you sang in Sunday school
or at summer camp.

The **JOY** of the **Lord IS** what makes you spiritually **strong.**

Our strength comes
when we have
the JOY of the Lord...

THE FRUIT OF THE SPIRIT

...in our LIVES.

If the opposite of **Strength** is the **lack of strength** – or **weakness** – then the opposite of **JOY** is the **LACK** of **JOY.**

If Satan is going to make us weak and ineffective, he's going to have to spoil our **FaiTH** and **JOY.**

That's why That's why That's why That's why Scripture warns us in Colossians 2:8

"....DON'T LET OTHERS SPOIL YOUR FAITH AND JOY WITH THEIR PHILOSOPHIES, THEIR WRONG AND SHALLOW ANSWERS BASED ON MEN'S THOUGHTS AND IDEAS, INSTEAD OF ON WHAT CHRIST HAS SAID."

Why? What?

Because if we let this happen to us, we will become weak and ineffective!

FAITH JOY = *weak christian*

A quick review:
How does Satan weaken a Christian?

By getting us to entertain ourselves with the empty philosophies of this world, based on men's thoughts and ideas, instead of what the Bible teaches.

Where do you find these

PHILO SOPHIES?

Who's Sophie?
No, no. It's "philosophies."

Television programs
Movies
Videos
Music
AND
Video games
are excellent

BREEDING GROUNDS.

Think about it.

If you were Satan,
what would YOU do
to weaken

a Christian's

FAITH
AND JOY?

First, you would **PRETEND** to Be the Christian's **FRIEND**.

I HAVE FRIENDS I HAVEN'T EVEN USED YET.

I'M YOUR FRIEND.

ARE YOU MY FRIEND?

I HAVE A FRIEND IN JESUS.

SHE'S MY FRIEND.

I'M YOUR FRIEND TOO.

Then you would try to poison (weaken) the Christian so he wouldn't be dangerous (strong) to you.

You would be clever enough to hide your poison by mixing It in something the Christian consumes everyday.

That's exactly what Satan has done to us! He has put his empty (poison) philosophies in much of our entertainment so we can literally **Entertain ourselves to death.**

☐ TV, iPod, texting, video games, cell-phones, music CDs, videos, x-box, radio, DVDs, HDTV, movies, constant facebook, my space—there's not much time left for this lad.

And Many of us

DO.

On a scale of 1 to 10,
How is your FAITH?
and the JOY of your salvation?
Just enough to get by?
Less than a ten?

Did you ever think that maybe God meant for you to be a level 10 Christian? Are you living for Him at a level 1 because you entertained the other nine levels to death?

The level 1 Christian hasn't lost his salvation, but is Satan winning the battle for his mind?

Do you see how this level 1 Christian is barely holding on to his

FAITH and JOY?

CHAPTER FIVE

I'm *NOT* saying
your salvation
comes from works.

We are saved by

God's
Grace

...and not by any works we have done!

I have always been a nice person. I don't mean to brag, BUT I...

✓ obey my parents...well, most of the time,
✓ never killed anyone,
✓ do my homework,
✓ am friendly to most people,
✓ empty the trash,
✓ make my bed...well, nevermind,
✓ mow the lawn,
✓ help old ladies cross the street,
✓ raked my neighbors yard once,
✓ gave a donation to charity,
✓ even told my sister I like her!

"FOR IT IS BY GRACE YOU HAVE BEEN SAVED, THROUGH FAITH — AND THIS NOT FROM YOURSELVES, IT IS THE GIFT OF GOD — NOT BY WORKS, SO THAT NO ONE CAN BOAST."

– Ephesians 2:8+9

But we have a responsibility to GROW spiritually!

If we don't grow, we will remain

SPIRITUAL BABIES

our whole life.

Now, that could be embarrassing.

Some people think
if they grow spiritually
in Christ, they will be
uncool and miss out
on all the "fun" the
world's system offers.

IF THAT'S WHAT
YOU'RE THINKING,
CONSIDER THIS...

When we see a baby in a crib that's just a few weeks old, she just lies there and coos, "Goo-goo" and "Ga-ga." This makes us smile :>) and say, "Isn't she CUTE?!"

"ISN'T SHE CUTE?"

But what if you went back
TEN YEARS LATER, and this
same baby is now
TEN YEARS OLD
and is still in her crib saying,
"Goo-goo" and "Ga-ga?"

Would you say this was
still CUTE?

OH, MY...

If you were *polite*,
you wouldn't
say anything
IN FRONT OF HER MOTHER,
but you would think
there was
something wrong
with this kid!

And you would be
RIGHT.

You see, we have a reasonable expectation **of seeing a child grow and if we don't see any growth, the assumption is**

Are you growing in Christ?

How would people RESPOND to you?

Are you **ACTING** your spiritual age?

WELL...DUH!
I'M LIKE,
TOTALLY
MA-CHER.

CHAPTER SIX

Try to imagine a clean sheet of paper.

The kind of paper doesn't matter as long as it is clean and usable.

Kind of like the next page...

Well, OK...so, that one's got a line around it.

It could be an 8½" x 11" sheet of copy paper or maybe it's the little note size paper that your mother uses...

...to write thank you notes.

What would happen to that clean sheet if you lit a match, blew out the flame and set the hot ash immediately on the paper?

P.S. Please don't try this at home!

These are professional match wranglers using professional-grade matches.

It wouldn't burn the paper completely, but it would scorch it a little and leave a little scar.

You wouldn't like it,
but you would
hardly notice
one little scar.

You still might
be able to write
a letter on it and
send it to someone
without anyone
noticing.

What would happen

if someone lit another match and set it down on your writing paper, and another and another and another, until the paper was covered with BURN MARKS?

Could you use it for a letter?

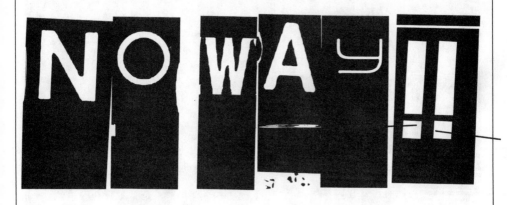

NO WAY!
NO WAY!
NO WAY!

WAY? NO!

There wouldn't be any

roomroom
roomroom
roomroom
roomroom
roomroom
roomroom
roomroom
roomroom

for a message.

116

Your mind

is like that sheet of paper.
Each scar represents sinful,
wrong thoughts and
attitudes that have
been burned into your mind.

When you accept
Christ as your Savior,
He comes in
and begins
healing the
scars with
the ointment
of His Grace.

WOW! A
CLEAN BRAIN.

As you allow Him
to control more
and more of your
life, He is able
to heal more
and more
of the scars.

This is called
spiritual GROWTH

But what if, as Christ applied the ointment of His Word to your scars, you continued to add more and more burnt matches by filling your brain (writing paper) with the empty philosophies of this world?

THAT'S RIGHT.

Very little progress would be made.

**He will
continue
to be in your life,
but in order for
PROGRESS
to be made,
you have to stop
burning your "paper"—**

YOU HAVE TO STOP
SCARRING
YOUR MIND.

When you accept Jesus as your Lord and Savior, the process of healing your brain (the renewing of your mind – Romans 12:1-2) begins.

".....DON'T BE CONFORMED TO THE VALUES OF THIS WORLD, BUT BE TRANSFORMED BY THE RENEWING OF YOUR MIND."

At the same time, Satan wants to weaken you and make you less effective for the Kingdom of God. Satan tempts you to keep adding "matches," but because you now belong to Christ **you have the choice to...**

...Just say, "No."

"You show that you are a letter from Christ., the result of our ministry., written not with ink but with the Spirit of the living God., not on tablets of stone but on tablets of human hearts.""

–2 Corinthians 3:3

WE ARE GOD'S WRITING TABLETS.

He wants to use us to send "love letters" from Him to the world. People are "reading" our lives.

IS THAT COOL OR WHAT?

WHAT DO THEY READ WHEN THEY READ YOU?

What is on your writing tablet?

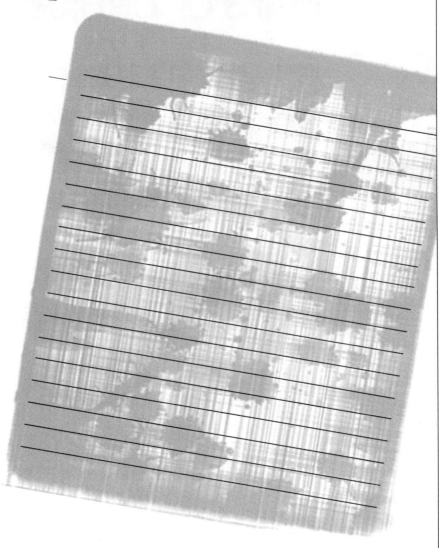

Is it clean and filled with His message?

Or is it scarred beyond recognition?

The Choice is yours.

Remember, life is
A SERIES OF CHOICES.

That's just choice.

What are you choosing?

What? Are you choosing?

Are you
askin' me?

CHAPTER SEVEN

Now maybe you're thinking that it's JUST a movie or JUST a television program or JUST a song or JUST a video game. How can THAT possibly affect my faith in Jesus and the joy of my salvation?

"I'm not joining in it. I'm simply using it to entertain myself for a while."

Please allow me
to respond with
a story of two little boys.

Billy and Bobby were
on a playground at recess.
Billy started telling a
dirty joke.
Bobby,
who was a
Christian,
wanted to
walk away,
but the
joke was funny, so he stayed.

He tried not to laugh,
but it was really funny.

"That wasn't so bad," he thought.

"And besides, I'm not the one telling the jokes, I'm just listening."

Then Billy told another dirty joke and Bobby laughed again.

When Billy saw that Bobby was laughing at the dirty jokes, he started adding profanity to make it more interesting.

AND BOBBY CONTINUED TO LAUGH.

Billy told another and another until the bell rang ending recess.

When they got to their classroom, Bobby raised his hand for the teacher to call on him.

"Miss Jones, Billy was telling dirty jokes at recess." Bobby proclaimed.

WHAT do you suppose
Billy said in his defense?

HA HA HA HA

"Yeah, but Bobby was laughing!"

HA

In other words,
"Bobby's as guilty as I am
because his laughter showed
he was actively participating
in what I was saying."

That's EXACTLY what Satan
is trying to get us TO DO.

IF SATAN CAN GET US TO LAUGH, CRY, GET EXCITED, TAP OUR FOOT, OR GENERALLY ENJOY HIS "TUNE" OR "STORY," WE ARE MENTALLY PARTICIPATING IN THE ACTIVITY JUST LIKE BOBBY.

MAYBE YOU BELIEVE THAT WHEN YOU PLAY, WATCH, OR LISTEN TO SEX SCENES, VIOLENCE, OR PROFANITY, THEY DON'T BOTHER YOU.

Why don't they bother you?

Ummm...well, I...ummm...

They bother God!

–Colossians 1:21

CHAPTER EIGHT

Much of today's entertainment media literally encourages us to become a nation of PERVERTS!

Before you jump ship from my logic, think about the following illustration:

What would you think of someone who spends his evenings prowling around neighborhoods, peering into windows, watching couples have sex?

Would you consider this guy a pervert?

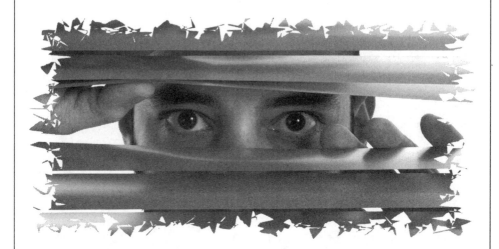

I would!

Isn't that what much of today's entertainment does to our MIND'S EYE?

PERVERT IN TRAINING.

It takes our mind into
other people's bedrooms
to watch them have sex.

Or into their bathrooms
to watch them
urinate,
PLAY WITH
THEMSELVES,
or get their PRIVATE PARTS
caught in a zipper!

This behavior IS ACCEPTABLE in
the world of entertainment
because it is "FUNNY."

Is it really acceptable behavior for you?

I thought we decided that PEOPLE who looked in on others' private matters were ACTING like PERVERTS.

PERVERTS
PERVERTS

Are you saying:

Is acceptable?

CHAPTER NINE

"**O**kay, maybe a lot of today's entertainment is PERVERTED and immoral, but I DON'T let it affect me!"

Add that excuse to "I just like the beat," and you have the most frequently used excuse by today's young adult.

"It doesn't affect me, you didn't see it affect me, and you can't prove it affects me."

No one ever wants to admit that their entertainment affects them in a negative way...

*I SWEAR...
IT REALLY
DOESN'T
AFFECT ME!*

I have

3

responses:

Response #1

HOW DO YOU KNOW IT DOESN'T AFFECT YOU?

God's Word doesn't say you'll be A PERVERT If you watch PERVERSION.

He doesn't say you'll be

if you listen to

music.

God doesn't say you will KILL PEOPLE if you play "FIRST-PERSON SHOOTER" games.

And He doesn't say you'll become a HOMOSEXUAL if you entertain yourself with HOMOSEXUALS

God's Word says...
if you choose
to entertain
yourself with the

EMPTY
PHILOSOPHIES

of this world,
you will struggle
with your
FAITH and JOY.

How is your

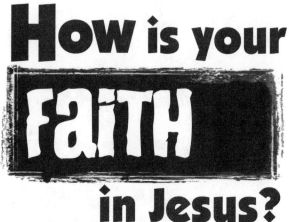

in Jesus?
Do you ever think
that you have lost
your salvation?

Do you ever wonder
if there is a God?
Is Jesus Christ God?

How is the JOY of your Salvation?

(Love, joy, peace, patience, kindness, goodness, faithfulness, gentleness, self-control, etc.)

and...

What are you ENTERTAINING yourself with?

(Television, movies, video, music, Internet, computer games, etc.)

Response #2

MUCH OF TODAY'S MUSIC AND OTHER FORMS OF ENTERTAINMENT ARE JUST LIKE A....

Commercial

THINK ABOUT IT!

What's the difference between a

Music Video

and a

Verizon, Volkswagen, or Victoria's Secret

commercial?

If you said about three minutes, you would be right.

30 seconds	**=**	**commercial**
3 ½ minutes	**=**	**music video**

In about 30 seconds, advertisers for

Verizon, Volkswagen, or Victoria's Secret

sell us their cell phones, cars, and underwear by using:

Music with
a good beat,
Cute girls, and
Fast video clips.

Does the girl
come with
the Ferarri?

In 3½ minutes, music videos use the same methods:

**Music with
a good beat,
Cute girls, and
Fast video clips.**

If Verizon, and other advertisers are able to sell you their product in 30 seconds, don't you think a video could sell you its product in 3½ minutes?

Yes, they can and they do!

What is their "product?"

It's the

PHILOSOPHY

of the
writer
and/or the
performer.

"But I'm not buying it."

Really?

 Reread response #1

Response #3

MUCH OF TODAY'S ENTERTAINMENT IS A VERY EFFECTIVE AUDIO / VISUAL EDUCATION TOOL.

Audio/visual equipment like:

Flat-Screen TVs, DVDs, mp3s, And especially Video games

are some of the most effective teaching tools used in the classroom.

When teachers use THESE TOOLS in a classroom, they can see learning taking place by their students.

**But what would you
call these tools
if we took them
out of the classroom
and put them
into your home?**

They would still be:

Flat-Screen TVs, DVDs, mp3s, And especially Video games

If they are effective teaching tools in the classroom, they are effective teaching tools in your home.

WHAT'S THAT?

YOU DON'T THINK THEY ARE TEACHING YOU ANYTHING?

No?

REREAD RESPONSE #1

CHAPTER TEN

I am **NOT** saying the entertainment media is the only way for burning empty and perverted philosophies into your mind.

It just seems to be the most effective way.

I'm **NOT** saying it is a SIN to  watch television, listen to rock music, or to entertain yourself with today's entertainment.

But...

When you do, be aware of the poison of

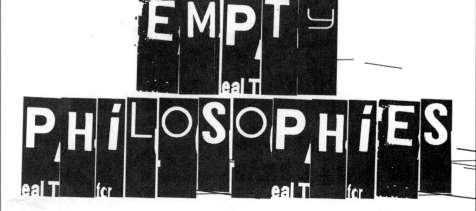

EMPTY
PHILOSOPHIES

that are being fed to you as a form of entertainment.

Psalm 19:14 says,

"May the words of my mouth and meditation of my heart be pleasing in your sight, O Lord, my Rock and my Redeemer."

What are you meditating on?
Is it pleasing to God?

Psalm 19:14

encourages us

to let our thoughts

be pleasing

to God, so

we will know...

His Peace

Is your heart at Peace???

CHAPTER ELEVEN

How can we obtain more PEACE in our lives?

- ✔ BY MAKING CHOICES THAT God WANTS FOR US.

- ✔ BY MAKING DECISIONS CONSISTENT WITH God's WORD.

How can we make wiser decisions about our entertainment?

Let me introduce you

to
The Teeter-Totter
Principle

A teeter-totter (or see-saw) is a straight board balanced on a fulcrum.

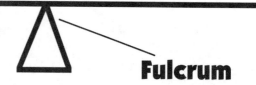

Fulcrum

Breadcrum

When weight is placed on either side of the board, it will naturally tilt to the side with the most weight.

On a spiritual teeter-totter, the board is our spiritual life.

The fulcrum is Colossians 2:8 which says,

"DON'T LET OTHERS SPOIL YOUR FAITH AND JOY WITH THEIR PHILOSOPHIES, WRONG AND SHALLOW ANSWERS BASED ON MEN'S THOUGHTS AND IDEAS, INSTEAD OF ON WHAT CHRIST HAS SAID."

This is the balancing point by which we can measure the weight / impact of entertainment in our Christian lives.

On one side of the teeter-totter are the empty philosophies of the world.

No Philosophy is emptier than the Satanic Bible.

The Satanic Bible
Anton Szandor LaVey

On the other side are the philosophies that bring life & peace.

THESE OBVIOUSLY COME FROM THE HOLY BIBLE.

The number #1 teaching from the Satanic Bible is

"Live for yourself. Fulfill your lustful desires. If it feels good, do it."

The next highest law from the Satanic Bible says to

Deny biblical values (deny Jesus)

Simply stated in five words,

On the right side of the board is the philosophy of Jesus:

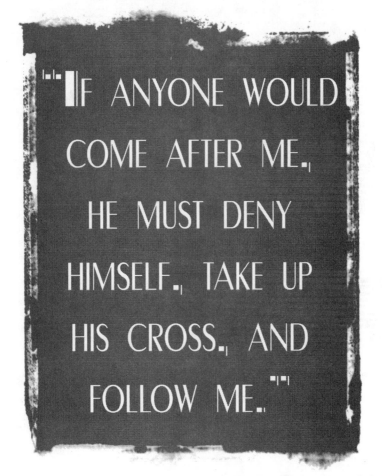

"IF ANYONE WOULD COME AFTER ME, HE MUST DENY HIMSELF, TAKE UP HIS CROSS, AND FOLLOW ME."

—Matthew 16:24

Simply stated in five words,

" LIVE FOR JESUS DENY SELF. "

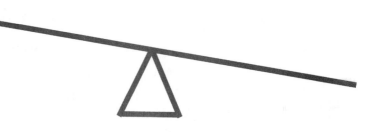

Can you see how the philosophies of the Holy Bible and the are total opposites?

| Live for Self Deny Jesus | VS | Live For Jesus Deny Self |

Where does your entertainment fit on the Teeter-totter of your life?

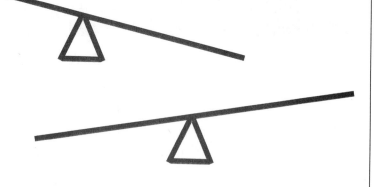

What are the philosophies of your favorite...

Music

Television Shows

Movies

Videos/DVDs

Video Games

?????????

Are they closer to the

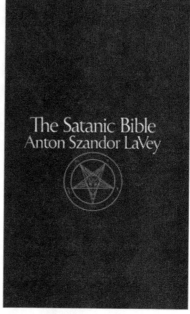

The Satanic Bible
Anton Szandor LaVey

or the

Holy Bible?

Does the philosophy and/or lifestyle of your favorite performer or movie or program or game feed your selfish desires or does it feed your soul?

Wow! Suddenly I'm very hungry.

Does your entertainment Teeter?

| Live for Self Deny Jesus | vs | Live For Jesus Deny Self |

or Totter?

Live for Self Deny Jesus | **VS** | **Live For Jesus Deny Self**

Jesus definitely carries more weight here.

You know how
a teeter-totter works.
If you put more weight
on one side than the other,
the heaviest side will
sink to the ground.

Some Christians think they are in balance if they entertain themselves with an equal amount of godly philosophies and ungodly philosophies on their entertainment teeter-totter.

The Bible says
that isn't balance.
That is spiritual
wishy-washy.

Revelation 3:16 says,

"Because you are lukewarm, neither hot nor cold, I am about to spit you out of my mouth."

If your entertainment teeter-totter is leaning toward the teeter side, there is a good chance your spiritual life is leaning that way as well.

That's why I Suggest Accepting A challenge.

The Fulltilt Media Challenge

CHAPTER TWELVE

Do you remember when you were a little kid on a teeter totter and the big kid on the other side would have his end on the ground?

Your feet would be dangling up in the air!

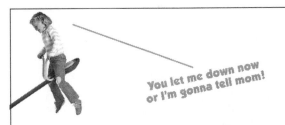

You let me down now or I'm gonna tell mom!

Only when your big friend got off, were your feet able to touch the ground again.

That's the principle of

THE FULLTILT CHALLENGE.

The FULL TILT CHALLENGE

- **It's designed to help you get back on your spiritual feet and clean up your mind.**

- **For the next thirty days, I challenge you to eliminate all music and other forms of entertainment that are against biblical values, and only listen to godly music.**

That's it!

Ya mean, that's
all there is to it?

I'm not saying everything else is evil. I'm simply saying doing this will help you see life from a more godly perspective. It's just common sense.

Can't I simply try to listen to better music and not watch bad movies?

You can, but you will probably continue to struggle with your faith and your joy. We need a simple plan and it doesn't get any simpler than this...

It's like

It's like going on a physical diet without a plan. You can say, "I've got to eat less fattening food" without knowing which food was fattening.

What I am suggesting is to eliminate all your "old food" (because much of it is "fattening") and only eat "new and approved" food for thirty days.

It eliminates all decisions and questions. It is our hope that after 30 days, you will be able to recognize which of the foods you have been "eating" are "fattening."

"But if I do what you are suggesting, isn't that...

A Form of Brain washing?"

umm...washing of the brain?
...with...brain soap?

Yes!

**When you
wash your brain
with Truth
it will help you
have a clean brain!!
Brain wash,
wash brain,**

CLEAN BRAIN!

See, I knew it!

At the end of
30 days of listening
exclusively to godly
music, see if you
have a better focus
to make wiser
ENTERTAINMENT
choices that won't be
poisoning your
Faith in Christ
and the
JOY OF
YOUR SALVATION

When all is said and done, remember the problem is **NOT** Marilyn Manson, Grand Theft Auto, and other forms of secular entertainment...

...and the answer is NOT

Listening to CHRISTIAN music.

The problem is Sin.

And the answer is Jesus.

Jesus Jesus
Jesus Jesus

There's just something about that name...

Your Entertainment can either help you focus on life from man's point of view...

...or it can help you focus on the

Author of Life

The Choice is Yours.

If you liked
this book,
why not share it
with someone
you care about...

...not someone
you think is wrong!

Why not sign up for the free online FULLTILT MEDIA CHALLENGE? It's free (absolutely no cost or obligation).

It will be delivered to your email for the next 30 days.

Sign up at www.AlMenconi.com.

For more information or teaching materials contact us at www.AlMenconi.com.